WHERE WE LIVED

STEWART ROSS

Wayland

STARTING HISTORY

Food We Ate
How We Travelled
Our Family
Our Holidays
Our Schools
Shopping
What We Wore
Where We Lived

Picture Acknowledgements
Chapel Studios 7 (top), 13 (top), 17 (top), 27 (top), Eye Ubiquitous 8; Hulton 7 (bottom), 9, 12, 13 (bottom), 15, 17 (bottom), 18, 19, 20, 21, 23, 25, 26; Mary Evans *Cover*, 4; Popperfoto 11; Sally and Richard Greenhill 22; Sefton 5; Topham 6, 16, 24, 27, 28; Wayland Picture Library 14, 29; Zefa 10.

Words that appear in **bold** are explained in the glossary on page 31.

Series Editor: Kathryn Smith
Series Designer: Derek Lee
Picture Research: Shelley Noronha

This edition published in 1994
by Wayland (Publishers) Ltd

First published in 1991 by
Wayland (Publishers) Ltd
61 Western Road, Hove
East Sussex BN3 1JD

© Copyright 1991 Wayland (Publishers) Ltd

British Library Cataloguing in Publication Data
Ross, Stewart
  Where We Lived
  1. Great Britain. Social life, history
  I. Title   II. Series
  941

  HARDBACK ISBN 0-7502-0142-8

  PAPERBACK ISBN 0-7502-1360-4

Typeset by Dorchester Typesetting Group Ltd
Printed and bound in Belgium by Casterman S.A.

Starting History is designed to be used as source material for Key Stage One of the National History Curriculum. The main text and photographs reflect the requirements of AT1 (Understanding history in its setting) and AT3 (Acquiring and evaluating historical information). The personal accounts are intended to introduce different points of view (AT2 – Understanding points of view and interpretations), and suggestions for activities and further research (AT3 – Development of ability to acquire evidence from historical sources) can be found on page 30.

CONTENTS

This picture of a London street was taken sixty years ago. The houses were built in the last **century**. They are small and the street is narrow. Would you like to have lived there?

How can you tell that this is an old picture? Look carefully at the houses and at what people are wearing.

These **flats** were built about thirty years ago. They were new homes for people who lived in old houses, like the ones in the last picture.

Many people do not like living high above the ground. There are no gardens for the children to play in. Flats like these are not built any more.

These houses were built in 1987. They have gardens, garages and many rooms. Are there any houses like these near you?

The way we build houses is always changing. Talk to someone who is about sixty years old. Ask what their home was like when they were young. This book explains how houses have changed in the last sixty years.

Do you have a garden? Dolly Miller did not have one until she got married.

'We got married in 1951, just after the **Second World War**. A lot of houses had been knocked down by bombs, so the **council** built new ones like those in this picture. We were very pleased to get a council house. It had a garden where my children could play. When I was little we didn't have a garden.'

7

Today many houses have gardens. Children can also play safely in parks and **recreation grounds**. But until about forty years ago, many children had to use the street for their games.

This photograph was taken in 1948. Why is it too dangerous to play cricket in the street today?

These houses were built in 1952. They have gardens at the front and at the back. There is a garage for the car too. How can you tell that this is an old picture? Look carefully at the car.

Do you have a living room like this, with a big sofa? The carpet covers the whole floor. Rooms have changed a lot since the 1930s. Ask your grandparents if they had carpets like this when they were children.

Today most families have a television. Some have a video recorder and a stereo as well.

Forty years ago, not many people could afford a television. This family was lucky. They are all waiting to watch a children's programme called *Muffin the Mule*. Their dog seems to be waiting too!

This picture was taken in 1945. Do you know anyone who was alive then? The family have just had dinner. Can you see the big dresser with all the plates on it?

The best room in many houses used to be called the **parlour**. Ellen Morris liked the kitchen better.

'We lived in a house that had only two rooms downstairs. I spent most of my time in the big kitchen. It was nice and warm next to the fire. We used the **parlour** when we had visitors. All the best furniture was in there; but I didn't like it much. It wasn't very comfy.'

13

IN THE KITCHEN

This woman is using a food mixer to make a cake. There is a microwave cooker behind the mixer. Microwaves cook food very quickly. In modern houses kitchens are often quite small. We don't spend much time in them. There are lots of machines to help us prepare food quickly.

This picture shows what some kitchens looked like in the 1950s. There aren't many machines. There is an electric water heater next to the sink. It heats water for the washing up. Can you see anything else in the room that runs on electricity?

In the 1930s not all homes had gas or electricity. This cooker is called a range. It has a small coal fire inside. You can see the shovel that is used to clean out the ashes from the **grate**. The heat from the fire makes the oven hot. Can you see the kettles keeping warm on top of the range?

Jenny Thomson remembers helping her mother in the kitchen.

'We had a lot of gooseberry bushes in our garden. I helped my mum pick the ripe berries. Then my granny came round and we all made gooseberry pies. The kitchen got very hot, with the fire burning in the range. I was too little to use the rolling pin, so I made the pastry into shapes.'

TIME FOR BED

Can you see a jug and basin in this bedroom? Some families had servants to bring jugs of hot water up to the bedrooms each morning. They poured the water into basins so that the family could wash. Where do you wash in the morning?

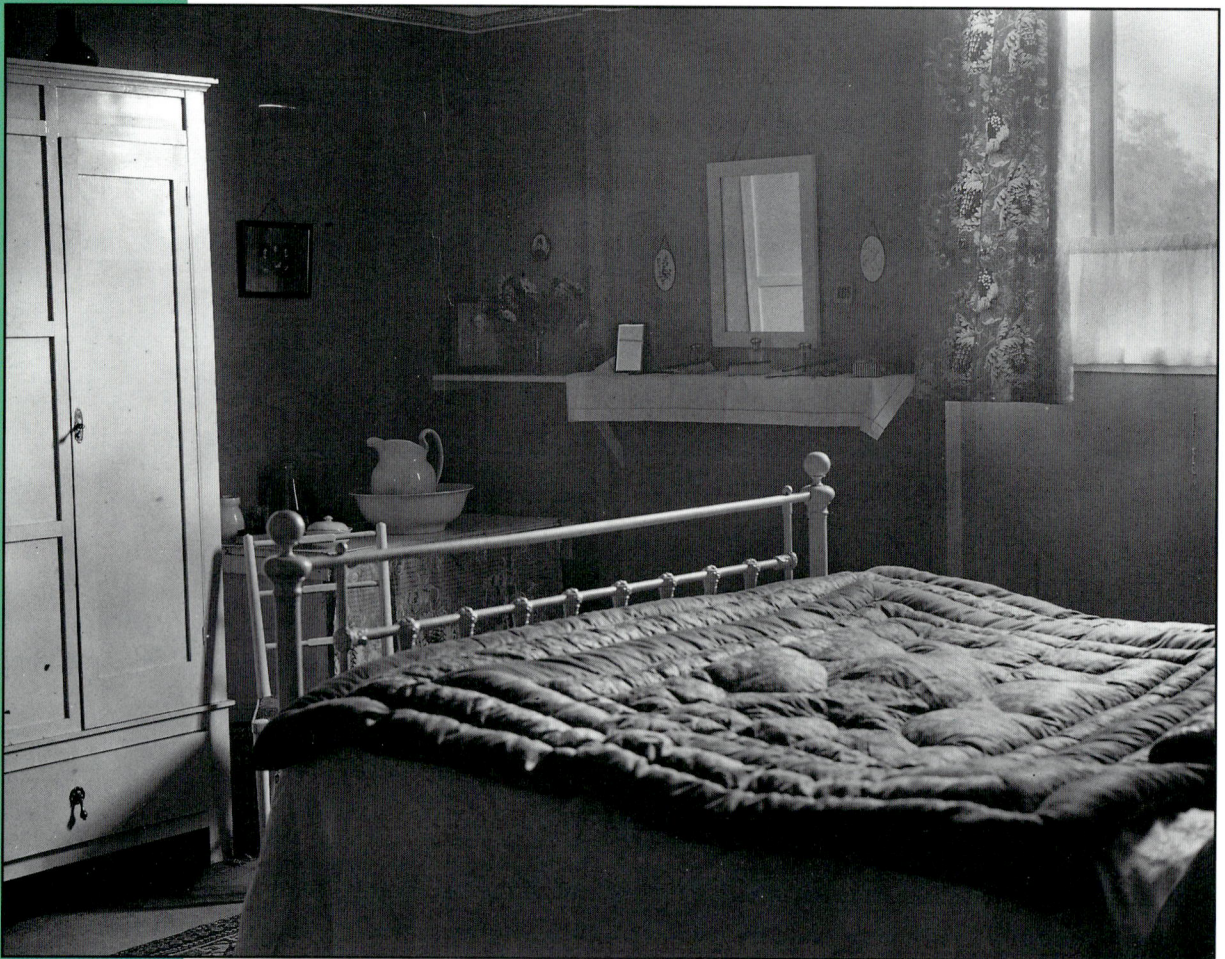

This is a child's bedroom in the 1970s.
Look at all the toys. Do you have any toys
like these? How is this bedroom different
from yours?

THE HOUSEWORK

This woman is turning on a gas light. Electric lights were invented over a century ago, but it was a long time before everyone had them in their homes. People used oil lamps, candles or gas lights instead.

Electricity is used to make all sorts of equipment work. Doris Green can remember getting her first vacuum cleaner.

'It was wonderful. Before I got my Hoover, I had to get down on my hands and knees to sweep the carpets with a dustpan and brush. Now I can stand up and let the machine do the work. Mind you, I think the edges were cleaner when I swept up by hand.'

21

You have probably seen a grown up putting washing into the washing machine. Washing machines make it much easier to wash clothes. Ask your granny about her first washing machine. How much did it cost?

In the 1930s, many people washed clothes by hand. This woman is rubbing clothes against a washboard. She is using a bar of soap instead of washing powder. Washing clothes was hard work and made your hands very red and sore. Some women did other people's washing to earn extra money.

How do you keep your home warm? Perhaps you have **radiators** or gas fires. About fifty years ago most homes had fireplaces in every room. Coal or wood fires burned in the fireplaces.

Houses were very cold at night after the fires had gone out. Every morning the ashes had to be cleaned out of the grates. It was hard work. The smoke from coal fires caused **pollution** too.

Look at the stove next to the gas cooker. It heats water. The hot water goes through thick pipes all round the house. This keeps the house warm.

The stove is about fifty years old. It still works well. Do you think we should stop using things just because they are old?

KEEPING CLEAN

This is a photograph of a bathroom in 1934. Look carefully at the bath and the toilet in the picture. How are they different from modern ones?

Until quite recently, many houses did not have bathrooms. People had to wash in the kitchen sink. Some homes had a toilet in an outside shed, called the privvy. Other homes did not have a toilet at all – people used a bucket instead.

Harry Wood was born near Nottingham in 1934. He lived in a small **terraced house** that did not have a bathroom. His dad was a coal miner.

'Dad was filthy when he came back from work – all covered with coal dust like the man in this picture. He washed in a tin bath in front of the kitchen fire. We heated the water in kettles then poured it into the bath. I can remember Dad asking me to scrub his back.'

OLD AND NEW

Many houses are hundreds of years old. People often think that old houses are better built than new ones. They think old houses look nicer too. Some of them have been **modernized**. The outside looks old but the inside is new.

This bathroom is seventy years old. It is still being used. Do you like it?

Here is a modern kitchen. Can you see some things that would have been different sixty years ago? Can you see some things that would have been different thirty years ago?

Do you think that modern houses are better than older ones?

Talking to people

Ask grown-ups you know well what their homes were like when they were children. They might be able to show you some old photographs.

Using your eyes

Look at the houses near where you live. Try to find one that is twenty years old, one that is fifty years old and one that is 100 years old. See if you can find some houses that are more than 100 years old. Why not visit a museum or old house which is open to the public.

Homes on display

You could make a history scrapbook or display about where people lived. See if you can find pictures of old houses to use. You could also draw pictures or make models of houses that you have seen.

Read all about it

You can find out more about people's homes by looking at some of these books:

A Century of Change: Homes John Foster (Hodder & Stoughton, 1990)

How We Used To Live: 1954–1970 Freda Kelsall (A & C Black, 1987)

A Century of Change: In the Street Paul Noble (Hodder & Stoughton, 1989)

Turn of the Century: Washday Ruth Thomson (A & C Black, 1990)

GLOSSARY

Century   One hundred years. The twentieth century, which we are living in now, started in 1901 and will finish in the year 2000.

Council   A group of people who look after a town. It is their job to find houses for people, repair the roads and make sure street lights work.

Flats   Homes that are in just one part of a building. Sometimes lots of flats are built together in a big block.

Grate   Metal bars that hold the fire in the fireplace.

Modernized   Rebuilt or altered to make something look newer.

Parlour   A smart living room used when visitors came to the house.

Pollution   Dirt in the air or in water.

Radiators   A flat metal container which is filled with hot water to heat a room.

Recreation grounds   Open spaces in towns and villages where children can play. Sometimes they have swings or playing fields.

Second World War   The war that took place between 1939 and 1945. Britain, the USA and the USSR, helped by many other countries, fought against Germany, Italy and Japan.

Terraced house   A house that is joined to other houses on each side.

INDEX